The Job Application Workbook

Michael J Lewis

First Published 2014

Michael J Lewis
Copyright © 2014 Michael J Lewis
All rights reserved.

ISBN:978-1505720051

The right of Michael J Lewis is to be identified as the author of this work has been asserted by him in accordance with the Copyright, Design & Patents Act 1988.

All rights reserved. This book is sold subject to the conditions that it shall not, by way of trade or otherwise, be lent, re-sold, hired out or otherwise circulated in any form of binding or cover other than that in which it is published and without a similar condition including this condition being imposed on the subsequent purchaser.

The Job Application Workbook | HOPE4Families

INDEX

Session 1 – The Product	4
Session 2 - The Curriculum Vitae	8
Session 3 - Writing the Letter	15
Session 4 – The Day of the Interview	21
Session 5 - The Big Presentation	25
Session 6 – Your Chance to Shine – The Interview	29
Session 7 – Making it a Success	35
About HOPE4Families	38
Become A HOPE4Families Partner	40

This course is for:
- Those who are struggling to get their first job.
- Those who are struggling to get the job they want.
- Graduates who are leaving University looking to get their first job.
- Those who are ready to take the next stage of promotion within their current job.

SESSION 1 – THE PRODUCT

The aim of session one is for you to understand that you are a product and that you have to sell yourself to the employer.

THERE ARE TWO TYPES OF PRODUCTS

What experience do you have?

It is important when applying for a job that you speak up about your skills, qualities and strengths that you can bring to the role.

Think about this example;

There are two types of products. Product one is worth £10, but there is no fancy case showing what the product can do. Product two is worth £15, but has a fancy case explaining exactly what the product can do. What product would you choose?

Most people, unless they have seen product one before, would always choose product two. What product are you?

Bearing this in mind you should be able to see how important it is that you sell yourself carefully to the employer, showing all the strengths that you can bring. You can do this on your Curriculum Vitae (CV) providing a record of your qualifications, experience and skills to the post.

TASK 1.1 – BRAINSTORM YOUR EXPERIENCE

In the space below write down things that will sell you to an employer. Therefore think about the experience you have gained throughout your life including your previous jobs, qualifications, hobbies, charity work and interests.

> What experience have I gained?

The Job Application Workbook | HOPE4Families

There are always a lot of people applying for jobs and you have to make sure you stand out over them. Spend a moment to think about these questions and write down your thoughts.

Why is it important to make myself different to other individuals?

_____
_____
_____
_____
_____
_____

WHAT DO ORGANISATIONS WANT FROM THEIR EMPLOYEES?

What does the employer want?

- Remember employers are busy and when scanning through CV's they are looking for people who stand out.
- The employer is looking for the best experienced, most skilled and the best value for money.
- They want someone who can fulfil the job description.

Remember when the employer looks at your CV:

- They may be reading through fifty or more CV's.
- They are limited with time to sit and read through everything first time round.
- It must stand out – **it must be concise, clear, bold, and different**.

Understand that you will be competing against:

- Cheap students straight out of University.
- People with over thirty year's experience.

TASK 1.2 - WHAT DO ORGANISATIONS WANT FROM THEIR EMPLOYEES?

Depending on your industry, certain skills are bound to trump others. But overall, what are employers looking for in an ideal candidate? According to research in 2011, Kent University has listed the top ten qualities employers want to see from their employees.

Carefully look through this list and number them one to ten. One being your strongest quality and ten being your weakest quality.

- Teamwork
- Communication
- Commercial Awareness
- Analyzing and Investigating
- Initiative and Self-motivation
- Written Communication
- Drive
- Planning and Organising
- Flexibility
- Time Management

TASK 1.3 – WHAT DO YOU NEED TO IMPROVE UPON?

Look back at the list above that you have just ranked and for your five weaker qualities write down one way you could improve them. For example;

Time management - I must prioritize my time more effectively and stick to deadlines I create.

1. _____
2. _____
3. _____
4. _____
5. _____

The Job Application Workbook | HOPE4Families

Session one notes:

_____
_____
_____
_____
_____
_____
_____
_____
_____
_____
_____
_____
_____
_____
_____
_____
_____
_____
_____
_____
_____
_____
_____
_____
_____

Homework:
This week begin to look and ask for opportunities to gain experience in a particular skill within your work place or job. Ask your employer for an opportunity to complete a project for free to improve a set of your skills. If you are currently out of work ask to volunteer at a local charity free of charge on a Saturday morning.

SESSION 2 – THE CURRICULUM VITAE

The aim for session two is to write an excellent Curriculum Vitae.

THE PURPOSE OF THE CURRICULUM VITAE

What is the purpose of the Curriculum Vitae (CV)?
- This is your brochure to show your skills to an employer.
- It is given to an employer in advance to try and secure a place at an interview.
- Remember, your CV is competing with many other people applying for the same job.
- A strong CV shows an employer how you meet their job criteria with your skills and experience.
- Your CV needs to be targeted for the job you are applying for.
- Your CV displays all your skills i.e. your sports, hobbies, interests. For example; playing football requires teamwork, commitment, discipline and leadership.

Complete your CV following this simple structure:
- Personal contact details
- Qualifications
- Training
- Previous employment
- Experience
- Hobbies and Interests
- Two references (One from your current job)

Make sure your CV:
- Has been proof read for errors and punctuation
- Has been spell-checked
- Has been printed on good quality white paper
- Has been neatly presented
- Is written in line with any instructions given
- Shows clear evidence of how you meet the job description and criteria

Why does the CV need targeting?
- Whilst you may have a wealth of skills across a range of disciplines, it is certainly not always the case that all of them are required for each potential position you apply for.
- Rather than present the reader with a sweet jar of bits and bobs to take their pick from, you present them with just what they require.
- You have twenty seconds to make an impact before your CV either goes in the bin or onto the pile of potential candidates. Targeting your CV will ensure you maximize your chances of going into the latter.
- Without the best CV you will not get an interview.

TASK 2.1 – WRITE YOUR OWN CURRICULUM VITAE

Using the clear framework below, add in your own information. See if this structure makes your current CV appear more clearly presented and easier to read.

PERSONAL DETAILS

Name: _____
Date of Birth: _____
Home Address: _____
_____
_____

Home Number: _____
Mobile Number: _____
Email Address: _____

EDUCATION

Higher Education (Start with most recent)

College/University: _____
Start Date: _____ Finish Date: _____
Title: _____
Qualification Gained: _____

The Job Application Workbook | HOPE4Families

College/University: _____
Start Date: _____ Finish Date: _____
Title: _____
Qualification Gained: _____

College/University: _____
Start Date: _____ Finish Date: _____
Title: _____
Qualification Gained: _____

Secondary Education (Start with most recent)

Sixth Form/College: _____

Subject	Type of Qualification	Grade	Start Date	Finish Date
Engineering	*BTEC*	*PASS*	*09/13*	*07/14*

Secondary School: _____

Subject	Type of Qualification	Grade	Start Date	Finish Date
English	*GCSE*	*C*	*09/13*	*07/14*

Other Qualifications

For example key skills, music grades, sports coaching awards, etc (Start with most recent).

Title: _____
Start Date: _____ Finish Date: _____
Course Provider: _____

Title: _____
Start Date: _____ Finish Date: _____
Course Provider: _____

Title: _____
Start Date: _____ Finish Date: _____
Course Provider: _____

EMPLOYMENT EXPERIENCE

Try not to leave any gaps in work history (Start with most recent).

Employer: _____
Role: _____
Date: _____
Description of roles:
- _____
- _____
- _____
- _____

Employer: _____
Role: _____
Date: _____
Description of roles:
- _____
- _____
- _____
- _____

The Job Application Workbook | HOPE4Families

Employer: _____
Role: _____
Date: _____
Description of roles:
- _____
- _____
- _____
- _____

EXTRA EXPERIENCE

Voluntary Work (For example at a local business)

Employer: _____
Role: _____
Date: _____
Description of roles:
- _____
- _____
- _____
- _____

Charity Work (For example for a local church or community project)

Employer: _____
Role: _____
Date: _____
Description of roles:
- _____
- _____
- _____
- _____

Interests (For example a sport, instrument, church, etc)

State your hobby and mention a skill it has taught you. i.e. I play football twice a week with my friends for a local club. This has taught me to be a good team player and has developed my communication skills.

The Job Application Workbook | HOPE4Families

- _____
  _____
- _____
  _____

Research Studies

For more advanced CV's you may want to add any research you have done or had published.

- _____
  _____
- _____
  _____

REFERENCES

Try to provide two references. One from your most recent work place and one as a character reference i.e. a professional that you know such as a teacher, doctor, accountant or nurse.

Name:	_____	Name:	_____
Title:	_____	Title:	_____
Address:	_____	Address:	_____
	_____		_____
Postcode:	_____	Postcode:	_____
Contact Number:	_____	Contact Number:	_____
Email:	_____	Email:	_____

Homework:
Get this typed up and ready to be sent off. If you do not have a computer pop to your local library. This is what gets you interviews, so make sure it is detailed and check your spelling, grammar and punctuation.

Session two notes:

_____
_____
_____
_____
_____
_____
_____
_____
_____
_____
_____
_____
_____
_____
_____

SESSION 3 – WRITING YOUR LETTER

The aims of session three is to learn how to effectively structure and write a letter of application.

WRITING A COVER LETTER

Every time you send your CV and letter of application to a potential employer you need to submit a small covering letter like the one overleaf. Whether this is by post or by email, the aim is to let the employer know what it is you are sending. They will use this as a first check to see if you are literate and able to communicate effectively in writing. So it is essential that things like spelling and literacy are very good or it might end up in the bin before they have even read it. Amend the one below to personalise it for your job.

The Job Application Workbook | HOPE4Families

TASK 3.1 – WRITING A COVERING LETTER

Your Address:
Line 1: _____
Line 2: _____
Post Code: _____

Their Address:
Name: _____
Line 1: _____
Line 2: _____
Post Code: _____

Date: _____

Dear Mr/Mrs_____ (*Find the name of the person you are writing to*),

Thank you for providing me with the details of the position advertised as a (*teaching assistant*) _____ at (*Radyr Comprehensive School*) _____.

Your advertised post of (*teaching assistant*) _____
is exactly the challenge I am seeking with more responsibility and accountability. I enjoy working with others and this role will give me greater opportunities to (*work with young people and help develop them*) _____.

Please find attached a copy of my curriculum vitae and a more detailed letter of application displaying the experience and skills I can bring to the post.

I trust I have demonstrated that I meet both your essential and desirable criteria and would welcome the opportunity to further demonstrate this should I be called for interview.

If you have any questions please do not hesitate to contact me at (*0784****893*) or email me at (*mike@bn*****et.com*).

Yours Sincerely,

Sign Letter: _____

Print Name: _____

The Job Application Workbook | HOPE4Families

LETTER OF APPLICATION

A letter of application is written to support your CV stating what you can bring to the job in more detail. It should explain the experience and skills that you have. In your letter of application you give examples that show how you meet the skills required to fulfill the job applied for.

Remember to always keep this letter formal and never write more than two pages. Remember your employer may have fifty or more to scan through so don't make it too long.

TASK 3.2 – WRITE A LETTER OF APPLICATION USING THE WRITING FRAMES BELOW

Your Address:
Line 1: _____
Line 2: _____
Line 3: _____
Post Code: _____

Their Address:
Name: _____
Line 1: _____
Line 2: _____
Line 3: _____
Post Code: _____

Date: _____

Dear Mr/Mrs_____ (Find the name of the person who will deal with the application),

Thank you for providing me with the details of the position advertised as a _____ at (this organisation) _____.

Paragraph 1 – Introduce yourself and why you want this job.

_____
_____

17

The Job Application Workbook | HOPE4Families

_____
_____
_____

Paragraph 2 – What strengths (key qualifications/experience/skills) can you bring to this job?
_____
_____
_____
_____
_____

Paragraph 3 – What work experience do you have that meet the criteria?
_____
_____
_____
_____
_____
_____

Paragraph 4 – What skills do you have that meet the criteria?
_____
_____
_____
_____
_____

Paragraph 5 – What projects have you done that meet the criteria? Can you write about a project you led, what you did, how you evaluated it and how you improved it.
_____
_____
_____
_____
_____

Paragraph 6 – What hobbies/interest do you have that meet the criteria?
_____
_____

The Job Application Workbook | HOPE4Families

_____
_____
_____
_____

Paragraph 7 – A brief summary of your key strengths and skills. Finish the letter by saying you look forward to hearing from them and working in that organisation.

_____
_____
_____
_____
_____
_____

I believe that I have the necessary skills to continue to raise standards at _____ and would relish the challenges that would be afforded to me. I trust I have demonstrated that I meet both your essential and desirable criteria and would welcome the opportunity to further demonstrate this should I be called for interview.

Sign Name: _____

Type Name: _____

Homework:
You need to take both the covering letter and the letter of application and write them up neatly. Again please check spelling, punctuation and grammar. Get someone else to read through the letter and make amendments if required.

Session three notes:

The Job Application Workbook | HOPE4Families

SESSION 4 – THE DAY OF THE INTERVIEW

The aims of session four is to help you to prepare for the day of the interview.

PREPARATION LEADING UP TO THE DAY OF INTERVIEW IS KEY

Preparation leading up to the day of the interview is very important to make sure you do as best as you can on the day. There are lots of things you can do to make sure you stand out above the other candidates and make a good impression.

The first thing you can do is create a portfolio to display all of your experience and projects you have been a part of in your work place. This will show initiative compared to other candidates who don't have a portfolio.

A portfolio should support your CV with evidence and contain the following:
- A copy of your CV.
- Copies of certificates (usually need to be photocopied).
- Tables showing courses and any continued professional development seminars you may have attended.
- Examples of any projects you may have led.
- Photos of you in the work place, your hobbies and experience.
- References that have been written about you.

Your portfolio should be presented clearly and colourfully. During your interview you can use sections of your portfolio to support a point or something that you are saying.

Secondly you can practice mock interviews to improve your technique for the day of the interview. You need to research the different types of questions related to the job. You can do this by speaking to another employer you may know, asking a line manager or researching on the internet. There will always be the obvious questions for example, what strengths can you bring to this organisation? You can always speak to an expert and get support with writing a good answer. You then need to rehearse and learn these answers off by heart so that they flow clearly during the interview. It is important to practice a mock interview in advance of the big day. You can use a family member, your current manager, a friend or someone you trust.

There are many other things you can do in preparation including:
1. Getting a map of where you are going for the interview. Drive there and see how long it takes at rush hour so that you can guarantee you are not late.
2. In advance ask for a visit and a tour of the work place so that you can get a feel of the culture. There would be nothing worse than getting a new job and not enjoying the work place.

3. Make sure you do your background research on the new organisation. When you arrive for the interview you can use your knowledge to impress them while making small chat in between interviews or during a tour of the work place.
4. Research and learn key people's names and positions.
5. Decide in advance what you are going to wear, so that you are not worrying about this on the morning of the interview.
6. Do you know whether you have to complete a one or two day interview? How long does it last? Do you need a place to stay for the night? Do you need to take a spare change of clothes?
7. Make sure the night before your interview you get everything packed and ready to go. You do not want to be extra stressed on the morning of your interview.
8. Finally try to relax on that final evening before your interview. Have a glass of wine, a hot bath and an early night.

Remember being anxious is a good sign, because it shows you want to do well. But if you are too worked up and cannot think straight then you will be no good for any interview. If you have prepared well, then there is nothing more you can do.

TOP 10 TIPS FOR DAY OF THE INTERVIEW:

1. **First impressions count**
   - Greet your interviewer with a smile and firm handshake.
   - Give good eye contact.
   - Try to make small talk during the walk from the reception area to the interview room and use the statistics and research you have gained about the organisation. This will show you have done your homework and are very interested in joining the company.
2. **Be prepared**
   - Re-read your CV and the job advert just before you enter the interview so that it is fresh in your mind.
   - Do your research thoroughly looking at the company website or by obtaining literature.
3. **Don't waffle**
   - Don't be afraid to take a few moments of thinking time to gather your thoughts before answering a question.
   - If you are unsure about a question ask them to repeat it. It is better to do this than regret it after the interview.
4. **Why should they hire you?**
   - Most job adverts will list qualities they want from the employee such as a good team worker or communicator. So it's up to you to think of examples of how you can demonstrate these skills in the interview.

- Have at least three strong points about yourself that you can relate to the company and the job on offer.

5. **Be positive**
    - Your interviewer will be thinking about what it would be like to work with you, so the last thing they want to hear is you complaining about your boss or current colleagues.
    - Interviewers like to see someone who enjoys a challenge and is enthusiastic.

6. **Remember your body language**
    - It is not what you say, but how you say it.
    - During the interview, do not fold your arms and lean back or look to the floor. Sit upright and try to maintain good eye contact. Use your hands and lean forward when making a point.
    - Many people cannot think and control their body language at the same time, which is why you need to have a mock interview and practice in advance.

7. **Expect the unexpected**
    - Your interviewer may try to catch you off guard.
    - Ask the interviewer to repeat the question if necessary but do not evade it.
    - Hopefully you will not be asked to dance to 'Blame it on the Boogie', like those job candidates were asked to do at B&Q.

8. **Develop rapport**
    - Show energy, a sense of humour and smile.
    - Smiling creates an infectiously positive atmosphere.
    - Always have one or two questions to ask your interviewer about the role and any issues the organisation may be facing.

9. **Clarify anything you are unsure about**
    - If you are not certain what they meant by a particular question, ask for clarification.
    - At the end, ask the interviewer if there is anything else he or she needs to know about.
    - Do not be afraid to ask when you are likely to hear if you have been successful or not.

10. **Remember your manners**
    - Ask them for a business card and follow it up by sending a thank-you email or letter, saying how much you enjoyed meeting them and how interested you are in the organisation. You never know when the next job might become available with them.

Remember to follow these three P's:
- Prepare
- Practice
- Perform

The Job Application Workbook | HOPE4Families

Homework:
Do you have a portfolio? If not it is about time you created one. Follow the previous instructions and make sure it is bright and colourful.

Session four notes:

_____
_____
_____
_____
_____
_____
_____
_____
_____
_____
_____
_____
_____
_____

SESSION 5 – THE BIG PRESENTATION

The aims of session five is to identify the best technique to approaching and giving an effective presentation.

WHAT IS THE PURPOSE OF THE PRESENTATION?

The more senior the job you apply for the more chance there is that you will have to do a presentation about your vision for the organisation. For some of you this section may be irrelevant for your first job or your current post. But as you advance in your career one day you will be expected to do a presentation as part of the interview process.

The employer wants an opportunity to see how you interact with the interviewing panel. They will make a snap judgment from this if they would like to work with you day in, day out. They are simply observing your character, your people skills and your presentation skills.

The key elements to a successful presentation:

- Preparation
- Do the research thoroughly about the topic
- Try and be the first to do the presentation
- Run it by someone before the day
- Make it look modern and well presented
- Speak loud, clear and keep good eye contact with all of the panel
- Smile more and try to look relaxed
- Don't jam-pack the power point with words – use it as a aide memoir
- Know that people have a short attention span so keep moving through your material
- Keep it short and concise
- Have a clear introduction, a middle and conclusion
- Don't assume they know anything
- Little amount of text and more graphics
- Laugh if you screw up and move on
- Look presentable

TASK 5.1 – MAKE A PRESENTATION

Create a sample presentation about your vision for McDonald's over the next ten years. Give your short term and long term aims to help make McDonald's a more successful organisation. Create a presentation to last three minutes.

Once completed practice your presentation in front of a mirror. As you read out your presentation from pointer cards look in the mirror to see your facial expressions. Practice this to make improvements and also to speak clearly and confidently.

Reflect upon your presentation skills and consider what are your strengths and weaknesses.

Two areas of strengths:
1. _____
2. _____

Two areas to improve:
1. _____
2. _____

Homework:
Now you have created your presentation about McDonald's, create one about you, including a few PowerPoint slides to go with it. You can create a rough design of a PowerPoint structure and find some smart graphics to stand out. By doing this you will gain some experience about creating a power point presentation and have some idea about what looks good and bad before you may be asked to do one in an interview.

TASK 5.2 - PEER ASSESSMENT TABLE

If you are following through this booklet with a group of friends or as part of a course then consider presenting your presentations in front of each other. While you present, get someone else to complete the table below to score you and give feedback (Score 1 to 5, 1 being poor and 5 being great). Use this to improve and develop your presentation.

	Person 1	Person 2	Person 3	Person 4	Person 5	Person 6	Person 7	Person 8	Person 9	Person 10
Good eye Contact	/5	/5	/5	/5	/5	/5	/5	/5	/5	/5
Spoke loudly	/5	/5	/5	/5	/5	/5	/5	/5	/5	/5
Clear speech	/5	/5	/5	/5	/5	/5	/5	/5	/5	/5
Concise points	/5	/5	/5	/5	/5	/5	/5	/5	/5	/5
Appeared confident	/5	/5	/5	/5	/5	/5	/5	/5	/5	/5
Passionate about what they are saying	/5	/5	/5	/5	/5	/5	/5	/5	/5	/5
Informative	/5	/5	/5	/5	/5	/5	/5	/5	/5	/5
Clear short term aims	/5	/5	/5	/5	/5	/5	/5	/5	/5	/5
Clear long term aims	/5	/5	/5	/5	/5	/5	/5	/5	/5	/5
Understanding of task	/5	/5	/5	/5	/5	/5	/5	/5	/5	/5
Did they sell you their vision?	/5	/5	/5	/5	/5	/5	/5	/5	/5	/5
Overall presentation	/5	/5	/5	/5	/5	/5	/5	/5	/5	/5
Total Score	/60	/60	/60	/60	/60	/60	/60	/60	/60	/60

Session five notes:

SESSION 6 – YOUR CHANCE TO SHINE

The aims of session six is to identify questions that could appear on the day of the interview and master them.

THE INTERVIEW

Every job you will ever have to apply for, will expect you to do an interview, although some will be more strenuous and formal than others. The key to doing well in an interview is preparation.

Your answers to questions must be;

- Concise and clear, don't waffle.
- Full of examples of what you have done to support what they want you to do.
- Confident. Keep eye contact. Look at all your interviewers.
- Thought through. If needed make a brief note of the question as it gives you a moment to think.
- Ask them to repeat the question if needed.
- Smile!

Questions are split into two main categories;

- Personal questions about you and your skills.
- Professional questions about how you can help improve the business.

TASK 6.1: WRITING ANSWERS TO INTERVIEW QUESTIONS

Below are samples of key questions that are likely to be asked in an interview. Remember there will always be more specific questions about your industry and specific role. If possible try and speak to someone who already works in this type of industry and get some insight into the types of questions that may be asked.

Please answer these questions using plenty of examples to support your points:

Personal Questions;

- What are your personal attributes? (An attribute is a characteristic, trait or quality of you i.e. Positive, hard working or reliable.)

  _____
  _____
  _____
  _____
  _____

- What professional development have you done in the past two years to make you a suitable candidate for this job?

  _____
  _____
  _____
  _____
  _____

- What do you consider to be your personal weaknesses?

  _____
  _____
  _____
  _____
  _____

- How do you want to be perceived by others in your department?

_____
_____
_____
_____
_____

Staff Supervisor/Management Questions;

- How would you manage a member of staff that is under performing?

_____
_____
_____
_____
_____

- How are you going to manage more experienced members of staff in your department?

_____
_____
_____
_____
_____

- How would you lead a team meeting?

_____
_____
_____
_____
_____

The Job Application Workbook | HOPE4Families

Leadership Questions;

- What is the difference between leadership and management?

_____
_____
_____
_____
_____

- What is your vision for the department?

_____
_____
_____
_____
_____

- How can you build a cohesive department?

_____
_____
_____
_____
_____

- How can you use data more effectively to improve your department's results?

_____
_____
_____
_____
_____

- How can you improve feedback to staff in your team?

_____
_____
_____
_____
_____

The Job Application Workbook | HOPE4Families

- How are you going to improve ICT in your department?

___

- How would you budget £10,000 in your department?

___

- How can you raise the profile and showcase your department to the public more effectively?

___

- How do you aim to bring in more business to your department?

___

The Job Application Workbook | HOPE4Families

TASK 6.2: MOCK INTERVIEW

You need to partner up with someone who can give you a mock interview. The more practice you have at this the better you will perform on the day of interview.

> **Homework:**
> - Type up your answers to these questions and add as many examples to support your answers. Practice saying them in front of the mirror and begin to learn your answers off by heart.
> - This week ask your boss for a mock interview. If you feel your boss would not do this, ask a close friend or a professional you know to give you a twenty minute mock interview. If possible film it and watch it back. How good are your presentation skills?

Session six notes:

_____
_____
_____
_____
_____
_____
_____
_____
_____
_____
_____
_____
_____
_____
_____
_____
_____
_____
_____
_____

SESSION 7 – MAKING IT A SUCCESS

The aims of session seven is to learn how to be the most effective employee. You now have the job and you now need to make a positive impression.

MAKING A GOOD IMPRESSION IN YOUR NEW JOB

You now have your new job and you want to make a good impression to your new employer. Please consider each of the points below and think how you can make a good impact.

Seven Steps to Success:

1. **Desire**

Only those who are hungry enough will achieve success. Success does not just happen you have to want it and work for it. Those who desire success and work towards it can achieve it.

2. **Decision**

Nobody achieves success by luck. Some people may get a lucky opportunity. But success comes after much hard work and commitment to a task. Hard work and commitment is a choice that has to be paid in order to achieve success. Therefore you decide to be successful. It's a choice, it doesn't just happen.

3. **Do It**

A lot of people want to achieve success but they continually find excuses and reasons to put things off. If you wait until you feel ready to get started you may never get started. It's easier to act your way into something, than feel your way into an action. If this is you, then be encouraged to go for it and chase your dream.

4. **Desperation**

In order to be successful you need to have a passion to see change. If you can tolerate the situation, you will not change it. In other words, if you are content with your situation you will never want to work harder and give more commitment to see the change and achieve greater success.

5. **Determination**

To achieve success takes focus and commitment. When things get hard, and they will, don't give up. Don't worry about what might happen, have a bit of backbone and press on. Worry is worthless; worry is the interest you pay on trouble before it comes. Stay focused on your goals and don't give up.

6. Discipline

As the saying goes the early bird gets the worm. Daily disciplines to doing things good will lead to success. It often means doing the little things others cannot be bothered to do. When you see others taking short cuts you need to do things right. It often means having the discipline to commit to what you set out to do.

7. Destiny

You may have a vision of where you want to be in three months, a year or five years down the line. You can achieve success and reach your dream. But understand, your future only holds what you faithfully do now. You have to stay committed to learning and improving in your role. You can do it.

Session seven notes:

ABOUT HOPE4FAMILIES

WHO ARE HOPE4FAMILIES?

HOPE4Families is an exciting, passionate, growing, not for profit organisation setup to help support families with marriage, parenting and financial difficulties. We try to help families throughout the UK build stronger foundations through courses, events, online support, help sheets, resources and partnership.

RESOURCING

Help Sheets and Articles
We provide a range of help sheets that provide information, advice and links about key topics. You can simply print these off and pass them onto friends in need.

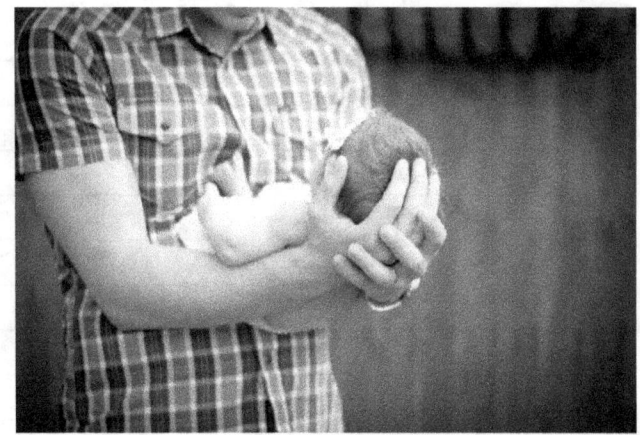

Workbooks
We provide a growing range of workbooks to develop basic life skills from budgeting to job applications, relationship support to parenting.

Leaders Manuals
We provide a large range of excellent leader's manuals for running our courses in community groups and churches.

CONNECTING

Useful Links
We provide an A to Z of 100's of useful links on all topics relating to parenting, finance and relationships. If there is a topic to do with families then you will find it here.

Helpline
We have a Family helpline open at certain hours during the week for people to contact us, have a supportive person to speak to, and to help be signposted to the best support for them. Please see our website for more information.

Social Media
Please connect with us on Facebook and Twitter @hope4familiesuk.

The Job Application Workbook | HOPE4Families

DO YOU NEED A SPEAKER?

HOPE4Families wants to help as many people in the UK build stronger families and marriages. It is our privilege to be asked to do a presentation about our cause, speak on a family topic of your choice or run an event. Please get in contact and see how we can help your church, community group or business.

TOPICS

Our topics include:

- Right foundations for marriage
- Marriage enrichment
- Expectant parents
- Becoming a stronger father
- Creating positive boundaries
- Parenting for babies
- Parenting for toddlers
- Parenting for children
- Parenting for teenagers
- Dealing with debt
- Learning to budget
- The Job Application

The Job Application Workbook | HOPE4Families

PARTNER WITH US

HOPE4Families Ambassador

We need as many people to be **HOPE4Families Ambassadors** and stand up in your church and community to let people know about us. We need people to raise the profile about the support we provide.

Please consider the following:
- Speak up about our work in your community or church. Invite us in to give a presentation.
- Fundraise (Race, skydive, cake bake, coffee morning).
- Corporate partnership with your business.
- Give a monthly financial commitment.
- Lead a course in your church or community.

Monthly Financial Commitment

Please support HOPE4Families with a monthly commitment and give to this great cause. If you believe family life is important, then please consider financially supporting us. Only with our partners can we run events, provide free community courses and support families who are in desperate need.

Please logon to our website www.hope4families.org.uk click on donate. You can choose to give a one off donation or signup to give monthly by direct debit. Thank you.

CONTACT HOPE4FAMILIES

- HOPE4Families, 171 Wyncliffe Gardens, Cardiff, CF23 7FD.
- info@hope4families.org.uk
- 0333 011 2222
- www.hope4families.org.uk

 Follow us on Twitter – www.twitter.com/hope4familiesuk

 Like us on Facebook – www.facebook.com/hope4familiesuk

Sign up to our newsletter on our website.

Book a Speaker

To book Michael J Lewis to speak at an event please email info@hope4families.org.uk.

Please look at our full range of workshops and topics available at www.hope4families.org.uk.

For more information about him please look on his website www.michaeljlewis.co.uk.

Feedback

Please email your feedback about this workbook to info@hope4families.org.uk and leave your review on the Amazon site.

Thank you.

www.ingramcontent.com/pod-product-compliance
Lightning Source LLC
Chambersburg PA
CBHW081804170526
45167CB00008B/3319